Discrimination in Society

Disability Discrimination

James Roland

ReferencePoint
Press

San Diego, CA

About the Author

After graduating from the University of Oregon, James Roland became a newspaper reporter, primarily focused on education. He later became a magazine writer and editor, as well as an author of more than a dozen books. He and his wife, Heidi, have three children, Chris, Alexa, and Carson.

For more information, contact:
ReferencePoint Press, Inc.
PO Box 27779
San Diego, CA 92198
www.ReferencePointPress.com

Picture Credits:

Cover: Elenabsl/Shutterstock.com

6: Gregory Reed/Shutterstock.com
9: annascreations/Shutterstock.com
14: Lisa F. Young/Shutterstock.com
19: BravoKiloVideo/Shutterstock.com
22: Dean Drobot/Shutterstock.com
26: BrankoPhoto/Shutterstock.com
29: Ajintai/Shutterstock.com

35: Maury Aaseng
39: Mark Kostich/Shutterstock.com
41: antoniodiaz/Shutterstock.com
46: SolStock/Shutterstock.com
49: Photographee.eu/Shutterstock.com
53: simonkr/Shutterstock.com
57: SolStock/iStockphoto.com
59: sportpoint/Shutterstock.com
64: Kathy Hutchins/Hutchins Photo/Newscom

LIBRARY OF CONGRESS CATALOGING-IN-PUBLICATION DATA

Name: Roland, James, author.
Title: Disability Discrimination/by James Roland.
Description: San Diego, CA: ReferencePoint Press, Inc., [2019] | Series: Discrimination in Society | Includes bibliographical references and index.
Identifiers: LCCN 2018019922 (print) | LCCN 2018021110 (ebook) | ISBN 9781682823828 (eBook) | ISBN 9781682823811 (hardback)
Subjects: LCSH: Discrimination against people with disabilities—United States—Juvenile literature. | People with disabilities—United States—Juvenile literature.
Classification: LCC HV1553 (ebook) | LCC HV1553 .R65 2019 (print) | DDC 305.9/080973—dc23
LC record available at https://lccn.loc.gov/2018019922

CONTENTS

The Fight for Disability Rights

Luka Hyde started second grade at Normal Park Elementary School, an innovative magnet school in Chattanooga, Tennessee. But he did not finish the school year there. Because he has Down syndrome, the school district reassigned him to what is known as a comprehensive development classroom in another school. This type of classroom is for students with disabilities and focuses much more on everyday life skills than traditional academic learning.

Luka's parents were not happy with this change. They contended that their son was being discriminated against because of his disability. They believed he would have benefited from remaining in a mainstream classroom. They took their case to court. In July 2017 a federal judge ruled that the school district had violated the Americans with Disabilities Act (ADA). The ADA became law in 1990 to prevent disability discrimination in schools, workplaces, and elsewhere in society. "The right to belong, the right to inclusion, and the right to avoid exclusion are all American civil rights,"[1] said Justin Gilbert, the attorney who represented the Hyde family. Luka ultimately transferred to—and thrived at—a smaller school with a more supportive environment where the focus was on the individual needs and skills of each student.

Speaking Out

The fight for rights and against the tide of disability discrimination has found advocates in all corners of society—from small-town family attorneys to the policy makers in Washington, DC. US senator Tammy Duckworth of Illinois is a champion of many causes, including better access to health care, veterans' affairs, and the rights of the disabled. As a combat veteran who lost both her legs during a mission in Iraq in 2006, Duckworth has a personal connection to these causes. Since her election to the US House of Representatives in 2013 and then to the Senate in 2016, Duckworth has led the fight to expand opportunities for people with disabilities.

> "The right to belong, the right to inclusion, and the right to avoid exclusion are all American civil rights."[1]
>
> —Attorney Justin Gilbert

She has also argued against proposed laws that would harm disabled people. In 2018, for example, she took a strong public stance against a bill that would make it more difficult and time consuming for people to challenge businesses that did not comply with the ADA. Duckworth said in 2018:

> This offensive legislation would undermine civil rights in our nation and reward businesses that fail to comply with the Americans with Disabilities Act, which has been the law of the land for nearly 30 years. . . . Passing it would send a disgraceful message to Americans with disabilities: their civil rights are not worthy of strong enforcement and they can, once again, be treated like second class citizens.[2]

The struggle to ensure greater access and opportunities for disabled people is not new. It has been going on for a long time in the United States and around the world. One of the earliest American advocates for disabled rights was Helen Keller, whose story was made famous in the play and movie *The Miracle Worker*. The

US Senator Tammy Duckworth is a champion of rights for the disabled. She lost both of her legs during a mission in the Iraq War in 2006.

story focuses on Keller—blind and deaf since contracting a terrible illness before her second birthday—learning to communicate with the help of a young teacher named Anne Sullivan in the late 1800s. After graduating with honors from Radcliffe College in 1904, Keller spent the rest of her life advocating for people with blindness and other disabilities. She appeared before Congress seeking more attention and assistance for the blind. And in 1920 she helped found the American Civil Liberties Union, an organization dedicated to making sure that individuals retain all rights and liberties guaranteed by the Constitution and other laws. This includes helping people who face discrimination because of disability, race, age, religion, and more. The organization continues to be a leading advocate for the rights of the disabled in the workplace, in education, and in other areas involving constitutionally protected rights.

Successes and Lingering Challenges

The fact that people with disabilities need such powerful champions speaks to the lingering challenges facing individuals struggling to overcome a wide range of physical or mental impairments. Certainly, many people with disabilities become effective advocates for themselves, asking for and even demanding fair treatment. But the fight for equality and understanding remains a mighty struggle. "Persons with disabilities are one of the last groups whose equal rights have been recognized,"[3] says Jody Heymann, a University of California–Los Angeles (UCLA) professor and lead author of a 2016 report on the world response to disability.

Despite ongoing challenges, there are signs everywhere that awareness of disability discrimination is improving. Employers, teachers, politicians, and other decision makers are becoming more sensitive to the challenges faced by people with disabilities. There is also a growing awareness that people with disabilities are often limited more by a lack of opportunities than by their physical or mental challenges. The more that educators, employers, and others witness the successes and accomplishments of people with disabilities, the more opportunities open up. "There's a growing cadre of companies that look at people with disabilities as an untapped talent pool," says Carol Glazer, chief executive officer of the National Organization on Disability. "When people spend their entire lives solving problems in a world that wasn't built for them, that's an attribute that can be translated into high productivity in the workforce."[4] There is still much work to be done, but learning more about how disability discrimination plays out in society every day is one way to start making a positive difference.

> **"Persons with disabilities are one of the last groups whose equal rights have been recognized."[3]**
>
> —UCLA disability researcher Jody Heymann

CHAPTER 1

Causes and Effects of Disability Discrimination

The ADA defines a disability as a mental or physical impairment that prevents a person from enjoying one or more major life activities. Disabilities can range from a mild learning disability that forces a student to take more time processing questions on a test to profound mental and physical disabilities that leave a person completely dependent on others for survival. Disabilities include those a person is born with, such as Down syndrome, as well as those that are acquired later in life, such as the loss of a limb in combat or a chronic illness that reduces a person's mobility, independence, or thinking skills. The ADA prohibits discrimination against individuals with disabilities in all areas of public life, including education, transportation, the workplace, and all spaces that are open to the public.

People with disabilities might seem to be a rarity, but they really are not. According the US Census Bureau, nearly 57 million Americans—19 percent of the population—are living with a disability. More than a third of US adults over age sixty-five have a disability, while about 6 percent of kids between ages five and fifteen have a disability. Disability affects people who are between those age groups, too. Among people with disabilities between ages twenty-one and sixty-four, only 36 percent are employed. In contrast, 76 percent of people without disabilities in that same age group are employed. For some disabled people, limited education and job training keep them from finding work. For other unemployed people with disabilities, it is hiring discrimination that stands in the way of meaningful employment. And for others, the disability is profound enough that holding a full-time job is just not realistic.

Robert Burgdorf Jr. is a disability rights scholar, law professor, and one of the authors of the ADA. He believes that most people, if they live long enough, will experience some sort of disability. Disability, he says, "will touch most of us at one time or another in our lives. . . . The goal is not to fixate on, overreact to or engage in stereotypes about such differences, but to take them into account." With that in mind, he adds, the goal of the ADA and other efforts on behalf of people with disabilities is to provide "reasonable accommodation for individual abilities and impairments that will permit equal participation."[5]

Roots of Disability Discrimination

The idea that people with disabilities need advocates and special legislation to make sure they have a chance for equal participa-

Pictured is a young woman with Down syndrome. Disabilities include those a person is born with, such as Down syndrome, as well those acquired later in life, such as loss of a limb.

tion in society may seem strange or unnecessary to an able-bodied person. But that is because the person might not realize the extent of disability discrimination. It exists in both subtle and not-so-subtle ways.

Disability discrimination springs from any of several sources. It might grow out of an assumption that a disabled person has far more limitations than his or her disability suggests. It might be a reaction to being around someone whose appearance or behavior makes others uncomfortable. It might be a matter of forgetting that there are people who need accommodations or special attention in all facets of living. Or it might stem from the unfortunate reality that some people's natural reaction to others who are unlike them is to be critical or insulting.

When it comes to physical or mental disabilities, many people hold beliefs that are based on stereotypes or mistaken assumptions. A common belief is thinking that a person in a wheelchair also has trouble hearing or thinking clearly. Danielle S. McLaughlin of the Canadian Civil Liberties Union explains:

> "As soon as a person is given a label such as blind, deaf, disabled, etc., society begins to make assumptions."[6]
>
> —Danielle S. McLaughlin of the Canadian Civil Liberties Union

As soon as a person is given a label such as blind, deaf, disabled, etc., society begins to make assumptions. This is as unfair as it is to make assumptions based on a person's race or gender. Remember when women couldn't vote? No? Well, the assumptions were that they were poorly educated, not capable of critical thinking, irresponsible, did not care and that the men in their families would take care of this important duty on their behalf.[6]

Pity and Courage

Uninformed assumptions often cause able-bodied people to view someone with disabilities as either heroic or especially needy, ex-

Is *Disabled* the Right Word?

Throughout history, many terms for disabilities and disabled people have been used and discarded. A hearing-impaired person who had difficulty speaking used to be described as *deaf and dumb*, while someone who could not walk was said to be *crippled*. For much of the twentieth century, the word *handicapped* was used to characterize a range of mental and physical disabilities. It is still used sometimes, most often in referring to parking spaces set aside for disabled people with a permit.

But *handicapped* and other phrases, including *mentally challenged*, have mostly given way to *disabled*. However, there is even some debate about the word *disabled* among people with disabilities, their caregivers, and others in that community. Some people prefer *differently abled* because it emphasizes ability and because the prefix *dis-* is associated with many negative things, such as disappointment and disfigurement. The term *accessible* is also preferred by many people when referring to bathrooms, building entrances, and other spaces modified or designed to accommodate disabled people. Typically, a sign on the front of a public building might have the ubiquitous stick-figure illustration of a person in a wheelchair over the word *Accessible*. But British professor and disabilities expert Tom Shakespeare (who himself has achondroplasia, a form of dwarfism) says that whatever words are used will eventually come to mean something negative if people's understanding of disability doesn't evolve. "Negative association will pin itself to any word," he says. "Changing parlance will do nothing if there is not a shift in attitudes towards disability."

Quoted in Rebecca Atkinson, "Viewpoint: Is it Time to Stop Using the Word 'Disability'?," *Ouch Blog*, BBC, September 30, 2015. www.bbc.com.

plains Sarah Blahovec, an advocate for people with disabilities. She says that these images are perpetuated by the media in news stories that portray the simple acts of getting dressed or making breakfast as major accomplishments or tell heartwarming tales like the high school football captain taking a disabled girl to the prom. Says Blahovec:

However, when it comes to real things that the disabled want to do, such as hold a job or participate in a sport, they (disabled people) are immediately seen as a liability. After all, if it is such an achievement for them to get out of bed every day, how could they possibly perform at the same level of a non-disabled person?

It is true that we should all be kind to each other, and the football captain who invited the disabled girl to prom was doing a nice, innocent thing for a friend. That isn't wrong, as long as it involves actions that are truly wanted by both parties (as opposed to unsolicited and unwanted help or attention). Kindness isn't wrong. What's wrong is that acts of kindness towards the disabled have become a genre of media that reduces disabled people to objects of pity or inspiration in stories that focus on the "heroic" actions of the non-disabled. We don't want that. We want to be recognized as regular people.[7]

Laurie Block, executive director of the Disability History Museum in Massachusetts, adds that thinking of a person as a disabled individual first, rather than simply another fully formed human being, is a form of discrimination. While it is true that stories about disabled individuals can be sincerely inspiring or can trigger feelings of genuine empathy, they become problematic when those stories shape society's broader view of the disabled community. "When tacit theories and assumptions such as these underlie public policy and social relations, they tend to limit the full humanity of those who are affected by them,"[8] Block says.

> "We want to be recognized as regular people."[7]
>
> —Disabilities advocate Sarah Blahovec

Similarly, able-bodied people often tend to view a disability as an illness that can be cured or at least treated sufficiently so that there is no longer an apparent disability. In some cases, that is true. A person with a mood disorder, such as depression, may take antidepressants and be able to develop a healthy lifestyle. This combination may be life-changing enough to allow the individual to enjoy a good quality of life, hold down a job, and have long-term, meaningful relationships.

But for many people with disabilities, treatments and lifestyle changes will have limited impacts. ALS (amyotrophic lateral sclerosis), for example, is an incurable neurological disease that weakens the muscles and reduces voluntary muscle control. Many other conditions are also incurable. Among them are total blindness, Down syndrome, and dwarfism. And while many people with mental or physical health challenges would gladly accept a miracle cure, plenty of disabled individuals view their disabilities as a part of who they are. They resent the message society often delivers that they are "broken" because of their disability.

Marie Harman has a rare inherited condition that delays development of motor and mental skills and causes muscle spasms and weakness in the limbs. She says:

> As a society, we need to stop looking at a disability as something that needs to be fixed. We need to stop asking the question, "What is wrong with you?" because in that person's eyes he or she may just be perfect. . . .
>
> My disability has led me to meet many wonderful people I would never have met without my disability, and it has given me a new perspective on life that one cannot truly know unless you walk in my shoes. I wouldn't have it any other way.[9]

Lack of Awareness

Disability discrimination is not always a deliberate act or the result of stereotypes or misconceptions. There are many examples of oversights that occur because of a genuine lack of thought about who might be affected or what services are needed by disabled people.

This situation is especially common in a classroom setting. Teachers who have not been trained in accommodating students with special needs may simply not know how to teach those students or what their schools can offer. Even simple accommodations, such as allowing a student with a disability extra time on a test or allowing that student to have a note taker in class, often go unfulfilled. In some cases it is because students are self-conscious about raising the issue, while in many situations, it is just that the educators do not know how to fulfill a request for assistance. Najaad Dayib, a student at Barnard College, says the problem can go much deeper—that some teachers seem unwilling to understand certain disabilities and the accommodations

Some teachers are simply not trained to teach students with disabilities. Even simple accommodations, like allowing a disabled student extra time on a test, often go unfulfilled.

they require. She has a displaced vertebra and other painful spinal problems that necessitate the use of a wheelchair. "I have been questioned heavily (by a professor) about an accommodation to the point that I gave up on trying to convince the professor and dropped the course," Dayib says. "The reason is ableism. Professors are either incapable of empathizing with your disability, or they simply prioritize their course and their way of doing things over your success in their course."[10]

Hospitals and doctors' offices are other common environments where the needs of disabled people are often overlooked. While these individuals may receive appropriate medical care, information is not always provided in ways they can understand. For example, when a patient is discharged from a hospital, he or she usually receives paperwork regarding follow-up doctor visits, prescriptions, and other information to make the recovery as successful as possible. A visually impaired person, however, may not be able to read a standard hospital discharge report. Complaints about this issue prompted the state of New York, for example, to pass a law in 2014 requiring hospitals to provide large-print paperwork or audio recordings that explain everything about upcoming appointments, prescriptions, therapy, and other concerns. Many health care providers willingly complied with the new law, but it was not until people with disabilities or their family members raised the issue that it became something that policy makers realized needed attention. Other states now have similar requirements.

Fear and Insecurity

Disability discrimination may have other causes as well. Many cases of prejudice against the disabled stem from what might be an innate fear or wariness of anyone who looks or sounds different from the majority. This has been true of attitudes toward immigrants and refugees from foreign lands, people of other races and religions, and people with disabilities. A growing number of psychologists and other researchers suggest that mistrust of or discomfort around people who are different may have its roots in ancient human societies. A person who looks, sounds, or acts different may be perceived subconsciously as a threat. Feeling uncomfortable around someone with a disability could be a form of self-preservation or self-protection. Even if there is truth in this theory, people have evolved well beyond primitive humans. People today have no reason to feel suspicious, fearful, or threatened by someone with a disability. That includes disabilities that might not be immediately visible.

Lynne Soraya, who blogs about life with Asperger's syndrome, recalls telling a supervisor about her condition and then being bullied and intimidated after her revelation. The supervisor's reaction seemed to stem from a sister-in-law who had bipolar disorder. "She'd had bad experiences with people she viewed as 'crazy.' Because of that, she now wanted nothing to do with me. She didn't have the authority to fire me, so she went out of her way to sabotage me. The fact that I'd been perfectly competent in the job prior meant absolutely nothing. The label was everything,"[11] Soraya says.

Feelings of awkwardness and tension around disabled people may also come from a place of concern or self-consciousness. In a British study by the disability advocacy group Scope, more than two-thirds of those surveyed admitted to feeling uncomfortable around people with disabilities. One of the main reasons offered for this sentiment was that they did not want to say or do something that would make the disabled person feel uncomfortable.

When many able-bodied people in a society are uncomfortable around individuals with disabilities, it can affect more than just one-on-one interactions between the able-bodied and the disabled. The mere subject of disability becomes an issue that people would rather not discuss, which often means that policy makers do not focus on disability rights and opportunities as priorities for funding and services. As a result, people with disabilities are not afforded the same level of respect as their able-bodied counterparts. "Awkwardness doesn't exist in a vacuum," says Frances Ryan, a British journalist and researcher who specializes in inequalities in education. "It bleeds onto discrimination and multiple forms of loss of dignity. There's a chicken and an egg to this. A society that doesn't steer its resources to counteract the

The ADA

While the 1990 signing of the ADA by President George H.W. Bush marked a turning point in the fight against disability discrimination, the struggle had been going on for decades. The 1973 Rehabilitation Act, a federal law enacted nearly two decades earlier, designated people with disabilities as a class of citizens who are protected from discrimination. The Rehabilitation Act banned disability discrimination by recipients of federal funds, such as schools, colleges, nonprofit organizations, and businesses that have contracts with the federal government. The ADA built on the foundation of that law, by prohibiting disability discrimination in all areas of public life. "With today's signing of the landmark Americans with Disabilities Act, every man, woman, and child with a disability can now pass through once-closed doors into a bright new era of equality, independence, and freedom," Bush said at the July 26, 1990, signing ceremony.

While the ADA has made things better for disabled people in many ways, it is still only a law. Getting all Americans to follow the ADA and see that it is enforced continues to be a challenge. Every year, more than twenty thousand potential ADA violations are investigated. About two-thirds of them are found to be without cause, but that leaves another third that have some basis in fact. Without the ADA, those bias cases would continue, leaving victims of unfair treatment without a strong legal basis to seek justice.

George H.W. Bush, "Remarks of President George Bush at the Signing of the Americans with Disabilities Act," US Equal Employment Opportunity Commission. www.eeoc.gov.

inequality facing disabled people comes from—and leads to—a society that doesn't view disabled people as equal. If you're not equal, you don't truly have personhood."[12]

Effects of Disability Discrimination

Not feeling as though they really have equal status with able-bodied people is but one brutal effect of disability discrimination. Disability bias can make life even harder when daily living is already a challenge. For example, a disabled person can go through his or her day watching others avert their eyes when passing in the street or listen as others complain about having to wait while a wheelchair-bound passenger needs extra time getting settled into a seat on a bus or plane. Tiffiny Carlson, a quadriplegic since suffering a diving accident at age fourteen, explains:

> Discrimination is a fact of life for many groups of people, but to be honest, I never really gave much thought to discrimination growing up. It wasn't until I became disabled when I was 14 years old when I finally understood what discrimination meant. It meant not only being misunderstood, but also being rudely mistreated. No one truly understands what discrimination is until they're on the receiving end of things.[13]

Disability discrimination does not stop with rude behavior or little day-to-day challenges. It spills over into the workplace and the financial well-being of disabled individuals and their families. Debbie Eagle, who has been visually impaired since birth, has a bachelor's degree in special education and volunteers teaching other disabled adults how to use technology. She and her visually impaired husband have struggled to find employment, and they sense that it is due to the stigma surrounding disabilities. Hiring a disabled employee can mean adapting a desk or other work space for that person's disability, or it can mean allowing that employee to have a modified work schedule to accommodate transportation needs or frequent doctor visits. "Employers are scared to hire us," says Eagle, "because they don't know what kind of accommodations we require. And if they don't meet what we consider to be reasonable accommodations, they're afraid we'll sue them."[14]

Fewer job opportunities translate into less income, which is made an even greater struggle if certain medical needs or expensive accommodations (such as a van with a wheelchair lift) are not entirely covered by insurance. Many adults with disabilities qualify for federal disability benefits through the Social Security

Poverty is more common among disabled adults than nondisabled adults. In 2015 more than 21 percent of disabled adults were living below the poverty level compared to 13 percent of nondisabled adults.

Administration, but in 2018 the average monthly disability check was only $1,197. Poverty is also more common among disabled adults than nondisabled adults. In 2017, according to the National Institute on Disability, Independent Living, and Rehabilitation Research, more than 21.6 percent of Americans with disabilities between ages eighteen and sixty-four were classified as living below the poverty level. That is in contrast to 13 percent of working-age adults who do not have disabilities.

Fight for Inclusion

People with disabilities are not looking for advantages over those without disabilities. Instead, the goal is to have an even playing field. *Inclusion* is the word often used to describe what people with disabilities want—to enjoy the same opportunities to get the same education as their nondisabled peers, have a good-paying job, enjoy a night of theater, and so on.

Discrimination against people with disabilities continues to inspire disabled individuals and their allies to fight for fairness in society. The battles are waged from local school board meetings to the halls of Congress. They are also carried out every day in courtrooms across the United States. One of the most expensive and time-consuming effects of disability discrimination is the growth of disability complaints and cases working their way through the court system. In 2011 ADA litigation represented one in eight civil rights cases in the federal courts. By 2016 that number had grown to one in four. Most cases are brought by individuals against employers. Many complaints are also directed at other entities, such as restaurants, hotels, theaters, taxi and transit companies, schools, hospitals, and government offices. These cases have led to millions of dollars in settlements and payouts by employers and others, though many of those who sue are not successful in court. The interpretation of the ADA and other laws affecting disabled individuals is often confusing and inconsistent.

What is clear, however, is that disability discrimination is a reality. And while it can be tempting to view the lives of people with disabilities as the real challenge, it is often their treatment by others that becomes far more burdensome. Rene Momene, a project coordinator with the Ecumenical Service for Peace and Human Promotion and an advocate for people with disabilities, adds that "contrary to what many might think, disability does not mean a poor quality of life. It is often the negative attitudes of society and the lack of accessibility within the community that are the real tragedy."[15]

CHAPTER 2

Living with a Disability

John Morris loves movies. In college he would go to the theater twice a week, enjoying his favorite vantage point about halfway up the rows of seats, right in the middle of the auditorium, so his eyes were level with the center of the screen. But in the three years since he became disabled and confined to a wheelchair, he has visited the cinema only four times. The spaces set aside for wheelchairs varied from one theater to another, but their placement always seemed like an afterthought, and never with the enjoyment of the disabled audience member in mind. Morris says:

> In many theaters, I have to park my wheelchair behind the row of seats where my friends are. Being split up from my group diminishes my experience, and makes for an awkward moment when we park to take our seats in separate areas.
>
> My seating location and viewpoint are important too, and oftentimes challenging to my comfort. If the wheelchair space is close to or directly underneath the screen, I have to crane my neck to watch the film. This can leave me with significant neck and/or back pain. If the accessible space is at the back of the theater, my view is potentially diminished by the distance from the screen. For those whose mobility impairments are caused by disabilities that are more significant than mine, the wheelchair spaces available may not allow them to see the screen or comfortably enjoy the experience.[16]

A diminished experience at the movies or other public attractions is a common complaint among people with disabilities. And though it may seem like a minor inconvenience to those without disabilities, it is just one of many examples of discrimination that can chip away at a disabled person's quality of life.

Improving Access

Improving access to movie theaters, restaurants, and other commercial establishments as well as to government offices, airplanes, and even apartment buildings is at the heart of federal, state, and local disability laws. Entrances to all buildings open to the public must be wheelchair accessible. The same is true for the public spaces within a building. Airplanes, buses, trains, and taxis must accommodate people with mobility issues. Outdoor destinations, such as Disneyland or national parks, must provide access for wheelchairs or motorized scooters.

These efforts have improved everyday life and enhanced educational and career options for people with disabilities. Judith Heumann, a US special adviser for International Disability Rights, a program within the US Department of State, has witnessed significant strides in the acceptance and treatment of people with disabilities. She explains:

I have seen a dramatic change over the course of my life.

I had polio in 1949, right after President Roosevelt had died. And when I was growing up, I was denied the right to go to school because I used a wheelchair. I only had a teacher who came (to my house) two and a half hours a week until I was 9 years old. I went to universities, but they were very inaccessible.

But now I work at the State Department, and I go to work every day on an accessible bus. I take the train home frequently. I fly on airplanes. I can drive—get on trains to get up the East Coast, and travel around the world, where conditions (for disabled people) are not as good as here.[17]

Day-to-Day with a Disability

Living with a disability means compensating in some way for the challenges presented by the disability. As with laws, advances in technology have improved life for people with disabilities. Technological advancements have found their way into tiny hearing aids, motorized wheelchairs, speech-driven computers, and medical procedures that are helping people live longer and with a greater quality of life than ever before.

But even with noticeable improvements through the years, living with a disability still means encountering discrimination in big and small ways. Because disabilities differ so greatly, there is no one common experience for all disabled people. There are, however, many shared experiences. Tiffiny Carlson is a quadriplegic who uses a wheelchair. She works as a writer and mentor to other women with disabilities. Though she has no cognitive problems, people frequently assume she has mental challenges, too. Carlson explains:

> Go to the grocery store, the movie theater, a store in the mall, a restaurant or any public-type place that has employees, and five times out of 10 you'll run into an employee who will automatically assume you're ill-equipped mentally because of an obvious physical disability.
>
> This happens to me constantly, especially if I'm at a grocery store with an able-bodied friend. Every time at check out, the cashier will always ask my friend if she wants paper or plastic [bags], directing all her questions towards her, never assuming I'm the one who's paying. Very, very frustrating.[18]

Carlson describes other commonly occurring examples of disability discrimination. Many buildings are still not ADA compliant to allow wheelchair access, and places such as concert venues or amusement park rides that do allow for wheelchairs often have quotas or limited spaces that frequently come up short of what is needed to meet the demand. "Very often when I try to buy tickets for a show, the wheelchair tickets have long been sold out, leaving me no option but to not go," Carlson says. "While this isn't considered illegal discrimination, in my eyes it is just as bad."[19]

Emotional Impact

Setting aside the physical part of having a disability, the emotional aspect of living with a disability can be even more challenging. For many people, having a disability may mean not having children or

Disability to Activism

When there are not reasonable accommodations in the public arena, disabled people are left with few choices—make the best of it, miss out on it, or work to make a change. Many of the people pushing for disability rights and greater access used their own disabilities as a stepping-off point to be advocates for change. It is not unusual to see the leaders of a nonprofit program aimed at helping people with specific disabilities have those same disabilities. It makes sense. They know firsthand the struggles of having a disability.

Elton Thomas is legally blind and a leading advocate in the United States for improving access to education and work for the visually impaired. He became an activist after learning how difficult it can be for visually impaired people to find meaningful work. "I began to believe that if the system could be changed or modified that it would be easier for people who are blind to get jobs," says Thomas, who began working for the Missouri Council for the Blind in 2009. "An active advocate is someone who speaks about an issue to someone who can make or support the changes that are desired. Similarly, an active advocate can be someone who works directly with a specific group to help successfully achieve their goals."

Quoted in *NewsInews* (blog), Medium, "Elton Thomas of St. Louis: Outspoken Advocate for People Who Are Blind," June 27, 2016. https://medium.com.

not having the career or lifestyle that they would like to have. It can mean being on the receiving end of other people's awkward sympathy or having others define you only by your disability. Disabled people often get stares from strangers, making them feel more self-conscious than they might already feel.

Eric Kenning is development director for the Arizona Spinal Cord Injury Association. He was born with a spinal condition that allowed him to walk as a child, but as it worsened, he was forced to rely on a wheelchair to get around. Along with the expected frustrations that came with having limits on mobility and independence, Kenning also grew angry at the discrimination he faced daily. People often turned away or pretended not to see him. Or they treated him differently from how they would treat an

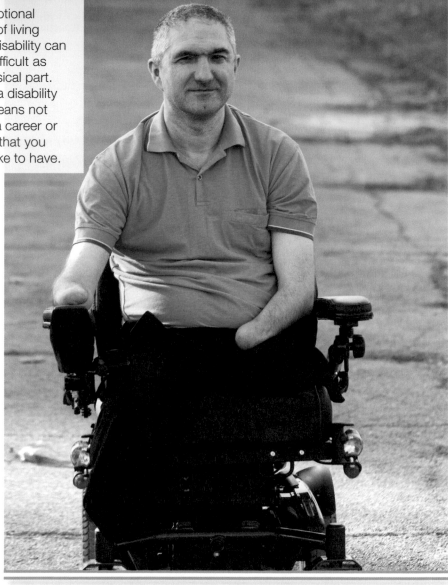

The emotional aspect of living with a disability can be as difficult as the physical part. Having a disability often means not having a career or lifestyle that you would like to have.

able-bodied person—and that angered him. He wants to fully participate in society—and feels he can do that even with his disability. But that is more difficult when others pity him or see him as needing special treatment.

To prove his point to friends, Kenning engaged in an experiment at a local mall: He intentionally bumped into someone with his wheelchair. Although he was clearly at fault, the other person immediately apologized—just as Kenning knew would happen. If an able-bodied person had bumped into a stranger, the response would probably have been, "Hey, watch where you're going." Instead, Kenning felt like he was not being held accountable for his actions—that he was viewed as somehow incapable of being a full participant in society because he is in a wheelchair. "That's where some of the bitter hatred comes from," says Kenning. "If society doesn't care about you . . . what am I supposed to do? How do I measure up? It's self confidence [that is affected]."[20]

These feelings can be particularly acute when someone who once had healthy physical and mental abilities loses them to injury or illness. Going through the transition from being healthy and able-bodied to being disabled can lead to resentment and bitterness, says Dr. Beth Sikora, an Arizona psychotherapist who works with patients who have traumatic brain injuries. She says the feelings can be overwhelming, somewhat like grieving the loss of a loved one. "They may realize they're feeling a loss of what they had hoped to be able to do,"[21] Sikora says.

Frustration and anger can also build up in people who were born with disabilities. Janis McDavid was born without arms and legs. He lives in Berlin and attends college there. He uses an electric wheelchair to get around and holds a stick in his mouth to lift T-shirts over his head so he can slip into them. He also writes with a pen clenched between his molars. Through the years he has found that a sense of humor helps him get through the dark moments. For instance, when crowds rush past him to board a city train, he is often forced to wait for the next one (and sometimes, even the one after that). And he would love to eat a meal like anyone else. Because McDavid cannot use cutlery, he has to take small bites of food directly off a plate. He can, however, use the portion of his right arm that he does have to balance a cup that must also remain on a table while he sips from it. "I could get upset about a lot of things," McDavid says. "But it wouldn't do me any good."[22]

Getting Around

The day-to-day challenges of living with a disability go down easier with a sense of humor. Jeff Charlebois describes himself as a sit-down (as opposed to stand-up) comedian. He performs comedy onstage but does it from his wheelchair, having been paralyzed in a car accident when he was younger. His disability is a frequent source of jokes in his comedy act. "As a guy in a wheelchair, I've found that humor breaks down barriers and provides brief moments of connecting to others,"[23] Charlebois says.

Even with a sense of humor and lots of patience, limited mobility can be a major source of frustration. "Taxis frequently avoid passengers with physical disabilities, not wanting to deal with our extra needs, seeing them as a headache and not looking at us as an equal customer," Carlson says. "Little do they know that we do not demand their assistance. Anyone with a disability hailing a cab solo can likely handle the entire transfer on their own."[24]

> "Taxis frequently avoid passengers with physical disabilities, not wanting to deal with our extra needs, seeing them as a headache and not looking at us as an equal customer."[24]
>
> —Tiffiny Carlson, disabilities advocate

But some people with disabilities do need the help of a bus driver, flight attendant, or someone else to help them get around. This can mean having to wait until appropriate transportation is available or having to patiently deal with people who may or may not be friendly in providing assistance. And if a disabled person is driving or being driven, there is the ongoing issue of disabled-permit parking space availability. These spaces are extra wide to accommodate a wheelchair or provide room for a person who may have a walker or other assistive device. They are located near the entrances of stores and other public buildings. Cars using disabled-permit parking spaces must display the permit so that it can be easily seen from the outside. Federal and state laws also require wheelchair ramps be easily accessible from parking lots onto sidewalks or to the entrance areas of public places. Ramps must also be in place to allow wheelchair access into the buildings themselves. Able-bodied people frequently take these precious spots. "The convenience is just too hard to deny," Carl-

Located close to building entrances, disabled-permit parking spaces provide extra room to accommodate a wheelchair or walker. However, there is an ongoing issue of disabled-permit parking availability.

son says. "And while this is all fine and dandy when it's in the middle of the night and there's no one else at the store, they generally take our spots in the daytime, especially the good ones that have extra room for our ramps."[25]

Disabled-permit parking spaces can also be trouble if someone parks there but appears to have no obvious disability. Emily Frye of Indiana returned to her car in a disabled-permit spot at her local grocery store only to find a nasty note on the windshield. A passerby saw her walk into the store and accused her of being lazy and unfairly taking a space set aside for someone with a disability. But Frye has a heart condition called tachycardia, which is an abnormally high heart rate that can cause her to pass out from exertion. "My life has been turned upside down," Frye says. "My family's life has been permanently affected. These episodes can and have happened at the most random times, sometimes while I'm simply walking, so I promise you I've more than earned a handicapped spot."[26]

And once a disabled person gets to his or her destination, there may be additional challenges ahead. Valerie Piro recalls a college visit when she was a high school senior. One wheelchair ramp was actually a sheet of plywood placed over a small staircase, and a button to call security for elevator issues in another building was broken. Piro says:

> Later during that visit, I noticed an elevator to get into one of the libraries, but it was too small for my wheelchair. As if I didn't have enough warning signs, I watched a student use his power chair across a section of cobblestones on the campus. As his chair bounced and jostled along the dangerously uneven surface, I wondered if I could withdraw my application and get a refund on the application fee.[27]

Opportunities to Participate

Sometimes disability discrimination rears up in some unlikely places or situations. This tends to be the case when the disability is not one that is obvious to others.

Mason Wicks-Lim, eleven, wanted to act in a Shakespeare play. At the time, Mason had a severe peanut allergy. Peanut allergies are defined as a disability by the ADA because they can be life threatening. Young people like Mason always carry an epinephrine auto-injector in case of a reaction to peanuts or similar allergens. Because of his allergy, he was initially denied the opportunity to participate in the Young Shakespeare Players East theater program. Leaders of the program said that they could not guarantee that an adult trained to use the auto-injector would always be nearby to administer the shot in an emergency.

Mason's mother offered to train the adults in the program, but they said no thanks. She took her concerns to the US Department of Justice. In a letter to the theater program after an investigation, the department stated that having an adult available to administer the shot was a reasonable request that could have

Hidden Disabilities

Disabilities are not always obvious. Some people with disabilities *look* healthy—or at least they do not have a noticeable disability. It is not uncommon for individuals with a hidden disability to be accused of taking a parking space not meant for them or to be given dirty looks for not giving up a seat on a bus or subway. Natasha Lipman is a British blogger who has a connective tissue disorder that causes chronic pain and joint problems. She carries an ID card explaining her condition. "Despite proof, some people only take me seriously when they see me struggling," she says. "I realize most people don't understand what they can't see, but my disabilities shouldn't need to be displayed to be believed." About three-fourths of people with a diagnosed disability do not use a wheelchair, crutches, or other adaptive device. That means that most people with a recognized disability may not appear to be disabled at first. But they need just as much patience and understanding as anyone else with a disability.

Quoted in BBC, "Hidden Disabilities: Pain Beneath the Surface," July 5, 2017. www.bbc.com.

been easily met. Jim Long, a former civil rights attorney with the US Department of Education, says:

> I think the letter is significant because it requires the youth program to provide affirmative services to the child to give him an equal opportunity to participate.
>
> This should serve as a wake-up call for all those entities that provide activities for children that they need to catch up and comply with the ADA—sports programs, summer camps, dance schools, cheerleading and tumbling schools, summer activity/sports camps, and so on.[28]

Mason's issue was resolved, and he was allowed to take to the Shakespearean stage. But the tempest that enveloped his struggle is an all-too-common fact of life for the millions of people who live with disabilities.

An Active Life

Disability itself does not necessarily sentence a person to a lifetime of unhappiness and unceasing frustration. "What many of us don't realize is that a disability is a badge of honor," says Charlebois. "It shows the world that we have overcome adversity, that we don't hide ourselves from the population, that we contribute to society. Every day we are out there fighting for a full and active life—a life that has not been easy on us—although most of us probably don't even think about our disabilities daily."[29]

Certainly, a disability that is accompanied by severe pain or discomfort makes daily life difficult. But disabilities expert Tom Shakespeare says that for many other disabled individuals, social barriers can often be more problematic than the disability. And rather than assume that a person with a physical or mental challenge must be miserable, consider that the disability may actually have positive consequences. "Sometimes, the part of life that is difficult brings other benefits, such as a sense of perspective or true value that people who lead easier lives can miss out on," Shakespeare says. "If we always remembered this, perhaps we would turn out to be more accepting of disability and less prejudiced against disabled people."[30]

CHAPTER 3

Getting and Keeping a Job

Months of looking for steady work turned into years for Jordan Gallacher of Pearl River, Louisiana. He is blind but has a college degree and advanced computer skills. (When he works on a computer, he relies on a screen reader, which audibly reads the words on the screen). Sometimes a promising job he applied for online will hit a dead end when there is follow-up paperwork that he is unable to read and fill out. "I'm always amazed at how many job applications I try to fill out online but can't get any further because the rest of the offline application becomes inaccessible,"[31] Gallacher says.

Curtis Everman of Longview, Washington, gets similarly exasperated with the time it takes to land even a part-time job. "I like to work fast and work my skills, but it takes a while (to find work),"[32] he says. Gallacher and Everman are part of a population of working-age adults with disabilities who struggle to find full-time or part-time employment. According to the National Institute on Disability, Independent Living, and Rehabilitation Research, only about 35 percent of people aged eighteen to sixty-four who have a disability are employed. This is a stark contrast to employment figures for the nondisabled population in the same age group, 76 percent of whom are employed. Breaking down those numbers even further, the unemployment rate for people who are blind or visually impaired is about 70 percent, and for people with intellectual and developmental disabilities, the rate is closer to 80 percent.

Low employment figures for the disabled are not due to a lack of effort by job seekers. The reality is that many potential employers choose not to consider hiring someone with disabilities. Their reasons are varied. They might have preconceived notions about a disabled person's abilities, be concerned about additional costs from having a disabled worker on the payroll, or feel uncomfortable working with people who have mental or physical challenges. "The unemployment rate for people with disabilities is outrageous," says Comcast executive and disability rights activist Fred Maahs, who was paralyzed from the neck down in a diving accident when he was eighteen. "And [the ADA] isn't going to change the attitudinal barriers. Probably at some point in their life, every kid today with some form of disability will encounter discrimination or stereotyping or bullying."[33]

> "The unemployment rate for people with disabilities is outrageous."[33]
>
> —Fred Maahs, corporate executive and disability rights advocate

The unemployment numbers are particularly frustrating, given that research shows disabled employees are, on average, just as reliable if not more so than their able-bodied peers. Studies by DuPont and other companies, for example, found that disabled employees tend to have lower absenteeism rates compared with nondisabled workers. In addition, disabled workers, on average, have lower accident rates on the job, and this includes technical, labor, clerical, and managerial positions. The research suggests that someone with a disability may be more aware of safety issues, not less.

Disability and Wages

But all that hard work does not necessarily translate to bigger paychecks. The median income for a person with a disability is about a third lower than that of an American worker without a disability, according to the American Institutes for Research. That figure reflects a disparity in the types of jobs that disabled people

People with Disabilities Face a Huge Jobs Gap

There is a huge employment gap between people with disabilities and people who do not have disabilities. According to the Disability Statistics Annual Report, published in 2018 by the University of New Hampshire Institute on Disability, 35.9 percent of people with disabilities (ages eighteen to sixty-four) had jobs in 2016. This contrasts with 76.6 percent of working people without disabilities in the same age group that same year. In fact, statistics show that this employment gap has changed little over time.

Employment Percentage, With and Without Disability, 2008–2016

Employment Rate With Disability   Employment Rate Without Disability

Source: University of New Hampshire, "2017 Disability Statistics Annual Report," L. Krause, et al., January 2018. https://disabilitycompendium.org/sites/default/files/user-uploads/AnnualReport_2017_FINAL.pdf.

are able to get as well as the typically lower pay they receive compared to nondisabled peers in similar jobs.

The job search process is often the first and biggest hurdle. It can be an enormous challenge for people with disabilities. The National Bureau of Economic Research did a nationwide study to better understand the state of disability hiring. As part of its study, the organization submitted fake job applications for a variety of junior and senior positions at various companies. The fake applicants for each position had the same qualifications. The only

Educating Employers

Overcoming disability discrimination in the workplace often requires some education of employers and coworkers. Some companies create an atmosphere of inclusion by voluntarily offering employee sensitivity training on issues such as disabilities and other sensitive topics. AT&T and other corporations have employee resource groups and employee networks to help promote disability awareness company-wide and provide disabled workers with mentoring and other forms of support.

In other situations, however, it has taken an employee's discrimination complaint with the EEOC to compel an employer to hold training workshops for managers and employees. These can be eye opening for employers, especially when they find out that many accommodations can be easily provided at little cost. But rather than wait until problems arise and this training is ordered as part of an EEOC settlement, Carlton Hadden, director of the EEOC's Office of Federal Operations, says employers should consider making training sessions part of their normal course of operations. "Proactive prevention is the best medicine to stop discrimination before it starts," Hadden says.

Quoted in US Equal Employment Opportunity Commission, "New Courses on Special Emphasis and Anti-Harassment Program Management," March 2, 2017. www.eeoc.gov.

difference between them was that some of the fake applicants included information about being disabled, while the others did not. Researchers found that the nondisabled job applicants were 26 percent more likely to gain the interest of employers. "Unfortunately, the results of the study do not surprise us,"[34] says Curt Decker, executive director of the National Disability Rights Network.

Decker says that one of the main reasons for employers to resist hiring people with disabilities is a fear of expensive and complicated accommodations in the workplace. But those accommodations often cost a lot less than many employers might imagine. Studies by the Job Accommodation Network found that 15 percent of accommodations cost nothing, 51 percent cost less than $500, 12 percent cost from $501 to $1,000, and 22 percent cost more than $1,000. Typical accommodations include wheelchair ramps, modified workstations, voice-recognition software, and adjusted schedules that allow for special transportation needs, medical treatments, or other acceptable circumstances. The federal government provides tax incentives for businesses that hire disabled workers and provides grants to help make accommodations. Nonprofit agencies also have funds to help businesses adapt their workplaces.

Bradley Beaumont, who has a spinal condition that keeps him wheelchair bound, believes that for many businesses, concerns about costs are just excuses. The twenty-year-old British man says that many employers underestimate disabled people who are determined to work. Beaumont is studying carpentry and has already advanced further in his studies than many people said he could. "I think employers know that (grants are available), but they just don't want to do it," he says. "I don't think they see what disabled people can do."[35]

Decker also believes that aside from financial concerns about making accommodations, many employers are simply prejudiced against having disabled individuals in the workplace. "There's still some stigma issues with employers," Decker says. "What's it going to be like to have a disabled person in my office? Will I want to look at them every day?"[36]

Discrimination on the Job

Even after someone with a disability has landed a job, there can still be discrimination and unfair challenges in the workplace. Other employees may not be welcoming because they fear a disabled person may slow down work flow or progress on a project. Or they may anticipate having to pick up some of the work responsibilities of their disabled coworker if he or she is not able to fully handle the work. Or they may simply be uncomfortable working with someone who is disabled.

Slights in the workplace or health-related complications can often lead hardworking and successful disabled workers to second-guess their work and their job security. "Enduring the stares and the obvious uneasiness of others, people with disabilities often feel painfully self-conscious," says Peggy Klaus, a best-selling author and nationally known consultant on corporate communication and efficiency. "Not surprisingly, they can lack self-confidence."[37]

While there are laws in place that prohibit the harassment and discrimination of disabled people in the workplace, that does not mean those laws are always enforced or that accommodations are always adequate for all disabled employees. Emeka Nnaka of Tulsa, Oklahoma, is paralyzed from the chest down. A football injury left him unable to walk and with limited use of his hands. Still, he got a college education and found a job with the United Way, sharing information with community groups about services for disabled people. But it is the little things that can make just getting into his office difficult. There is no button to automatically open the doors from the outside, for example. This means a person unable to pull a door open must wait for someone else to come along and open the door. ADA guidelines recommend such a system, but it is not required. Motoring his wheelchair into the elevator, Nnaka finds it is too narrow for him to turn his chair around so he can press the button for his floor. Again, he has to wait for a stranger to help him out.

Couple those logistical challenges with myriad other employment and access issues, and the goals of the ADA still seem a long way from being realized. Nnaka explains, "There's so much more that people with disabilities need, to be inclusive and included in this society. To have just the same opportunity that anybody else has."[38]

There is no single reason for job-related disability discrimination, and in time the solutions for people such as Nnaka, Gallacher, and others may be readily available and be accessible

Office buildings often lack basic accommodations for disabled employees. For many disabled workers, just opening the front door of the building can be a struggle.

without having to struggle or even ask. But it is going to take time, says Michael Morris, executive director of the National Disability Institute in Washington, DC. "Attitudes change slowly," he says, adding that employers who hire disabled workers and help them succeed in their jobs realize that hiring people with disabilities can be a very positive experience. He points to internships for college students with disabilities that are giving employers firsthand experience with these hardworking individuals. "That actual experience does more to change attitudes, change perception, right through to their HR offices that say, 'Wow, hidden talent pool. Let's explore it,'"[39] says Morris.

Sharing Personal Information

People who have disabilities that are not visible to the rest of the world sometimes wrestle with whether to share information about their condition with supervisors and coworkers. Some employees want to be up front because there will be workplace accommodations necessary to do the job or there may be times when doctor appointments will require time away from work. If no special workplace accommodations are needed, a person with a well-managed or minor disability might not want to disclose any disability information.

Lynne Soraya blogs about having a form of autism called Asperger's syndrome. She has found it helpful to tell close friends about her condition and some of its effects, which include depression and anxiety. Knowing this about Soraya has helped those friends understand why she might not always pick up on nonverbal cues or why she sometimes gets agitated when there are minor changes to a plan or situation. Knowing her friends understood the signs of Asperger's syndrome made Soraya feel less self-conscious and more willing to be herself. Thinking that sharing this type of information with her supervisor at work might have similar benefits, she initiated a conversation with her. Soraya explained that she might occasionally need to take breaks from work to deal with her depression. The conversation did not go well. The supervisor made Soraya's life at work miserable. In an effort to make Soraya appear incompetent as a result of her challenges, the supervisor falsified information and portrayed Soraya to others as unfit for the job. "Rather than endure the stress of her bullying on top of my existing issues, I gave my notice," Soraya says. "The experience shaped me very strongly, and I learned to mask my disabilities and their related consequences in order to survive. Depression was a weakness that you dared not admit: it could lose you your job."[40]

The question of whether to share disability information is an even trickier question when looking for a job. Some people want to be completely up front when submitting a résumé or job application. Part of that stems from not wanting to surprise an employer at a job interview. But many people who specialize in helping disabled individuals find work say job seekers should focus more on whether the job is a good fit at first, and then consider how much personal information to share. "The first thing job seekers need to ask themselves is, 'Can I do the job?'" says Jonathan Kaufman, president of DisabilityWorks. "If the answer is yes and the disability doesn't affect job performance, then don't mention it."[41] Dr. Daniel J. Ryan, author of *Job Search Handbook for People with Disabilities* and director of career planning at the State University of New York at Buffalo, agrees. "Employers use resumes to weed people out, so anything on the resume that would allude to a disability—given the realities of the marketplace—will probably work against you,"[42] Ryan says.

Job search experts recommend that disabled people not mention their disabilities in a job interview unless they feel it will impact their ability to do the job successfully.

The Limits of Changing Attitudes Through Laws

The passage of the ADA in 1990 was meant to break down barriers to hiring and to combat workplace discrimination. Before that time, disabled individuals who felt they were treated unfairly in the hiring process or who were denied promotions, fired without cause, or otherwise deprived of fair and reasonable working conditions had few options. Job-related complaints could be filed with a company's human resources department or with state agencies that investigated civil rights abuses. But the ADA gave disabled people federal protections against discrimination in the workplace.

Having a law in place does not always mean it will be enforced properly everywhere. For the ADA to truly help the people it was in-

Employers Also Have Rights in Discrimination Cases

People with disabilities have certain rights under the law but so do employers. Employers who can show that they had a compelling reason for their decisions or actions may prevail in court. This is what happened in the case of one company that owns and runs restaurants. In April 2018 a federal appeals court judge ruled in the company's favor after a manager complained of disability discrimination. The case stemmed from events that took place when the restaurant manager was depositing the restaurant's money at the end of a shift. He was robbed at gunpoint, hit on the head, and his car was stolen. In the months that followed, the manager said he experienced serious PTSD symptoms and depression. He asked to be excused from his employer's requirement that all managers work rotating shifts (days and evenings). The employee claimed working a combination of day and night shifts worsened his PTSD. The company refused his request, prompting the manager to file a discrimination complaint.

The restaurant company argued that working rotating shifts was an essential function of the job and that by allowing this manager to skip that requirement, scheduling problems and other complications would result. During questioning, the employee agreed that rotating shifts were essential to the job. So even though the employee was a sympathetic figure, the court noted that the law clearly states that discrimination complaints cannot be upheld if a worker is no longer able to perform an indisputably essential part of the job.

tended to, employers and decision makers must embrace the spirit of the law and be willing to commit the dollars and time to make it work. And for people who hold prejudices against the disabled, it will take more than a law passed in Washington, DC, to change those views. "What the law did not do was to remove attitudinal barriers," says Philip Kahn-Pauli, the policy and practices director of RespectAbility, a nonprofit group that works to advance opportunities for people with disabilities. "You can make explicit discrimination illegal, but you can't change people's hearts and minds."[43]

In some ways, the ADA may have inadvertently discouraged some employers from hiring disabled workers. That is because the legislation meant employers would have to provide workplace accommodations, which can cost an employer money. And then if those accommodations are not provided in a timely manner, the ADA can be used as the basis of a lawsuit against the employer. That has been happening more and more. In 2016 more than nine thousand ADA-related cases were filed in federal district courts around the country—up from about seven thousand the year before.

Typically, if a disabled person believes he or she has been treated unfairly, that person is supposed to take the issue up with a supervisor or with human resources. If the problem is not resolved internally, the employee can file a claim with the US Equal Employment Opportunity Commission (EEOC), a government agency created to help ensure fair treatment of workers and to deal with workplace complaints related to race, religion, disability, and other similar matters.

Turning to the EEOC

EEOC cases include complaints brought against international corporations and local companies, as well as federal and small-town governmental agencies. As an example, in 2006 a man who worked for Lowe's, a national hardware store chain, was hired as a customer service representative. A spinal cord injury that caused him to have limited use of his right arm did not impede his hiring, nor did it prevent him from being promoted to department manager. He held that job successfully for six years. Because of his disability, he was unable to handle power tools that required two hands. But he was able to delegate those responsibilities to other employees and, at the time, that was considered a reasonable workplace accommodation. He was eventually demoted and had his pay significantly cut because the company no longer supported these actions. The man took his case to the EEOC. "They (employers) do not think about disability," Kahn-Pauli says. "What they may not recognize is that disability is a natural part of the human experience and cuts across other barriers that divide us."[44]

CHAPTER 4

Challenges in Education

When it comes to the fight for a quality education for young people with disabilities, the battle is often waged by parents who have discovered schools discriminating against their children. It can be an exhausting struggle. State and federal laws require schools to provide an adequate education for all of their students, regardless of a student's special needs. But services can vary greatly both within and between school districts.

Kelly Fischer of New Orleans learned some difficult lessons trying to find a school for her son Noah, who has developmental disabilities that place him well behind his peers in terms of academic performance. He also needs help with basic functions like going to the bathroom and eating lunch. Fischer quickly grew disillusioned when she approached schools in her community, asking if they could accommodate her twelve-year-old son. Many school officials openly admitted they were not interested in enrolling Noah and providing the services he required. "When someone says, 'We're not a good fit for you,' it's basically saying, 'We don't have what you need,'" Fischer says. "When a school tells you what they don't have and it's something that your child currently requires, that would be like a regular-ed program saying, 'We don't have textbooks here' or 'We don't have teachers here.' Why would you apply?"[45]

Fischer eventually found a school that was a great fit for Noah, but not before she joined other families in a class-action lawsuit against the school district. It was just one of many such lawsuits the Southern Poverty Law Center (SPLC) files annually on behalf of parents fighting disability discrimination in schools. "The thing that just concerns me is why is it possible that this school can meet the law and others can't?" Fischer says. "Why was I so shocked to come across such a good program, which is basically a program that does what a school is supposed to do? I shouldn't have been shocked about that. That should have been everywhere."[46]

How Many Students Are Disabled?

Having to provide services and special education programs is not an uncommon expectation for schools across the country. An es-

An estimated 6.5 million young people have a disability. However, some disabilities, such as limited use of arms or legs, may have little or no effect on learning and academic success.

timated 6.5 million young people ages three to twenty-one have a disability, according to the National Center for Education Statistics. That is about 13 percent of this age group. The percentage is the same regardless of gender, race, and geographic location.

Some disabilities, such as limited use of an arm or leg due to a medical condition or injury, may have little or no effect on learning and academic success. A child with a congenital heart condition, for example, may not be able to participate in typical physical education classes or compete in contact sports but may get good grades and have an otherwise well-rounded and enjoyable school career.

But many of those 6.5 million young people with a disability find that their challenges have a significant effect on their school experience. A student who requires ongoing medical care, such as dialysis for kidney disease, may face problems related to multiple absences. Apart from students with chronic health conditions, more than a third of students receiving special education services have a specific learning disability. Some common types of learning disabilities include the following:

- Dyslexia: The brain interprets letters, words, numbers, and symbols abnormally, affecting reading comprehension, writing, speech, recall, and other aspects of learning.

- Auditory processing disorder: A learning challenge that occurs when sound travels normally through the ear but is interpreted incorrectly by the brain.

- Dysgraphia: Difficulty with writing and other small-motor tasks.

- Nonverbal learning disabilities: A disorder in which higher verbal skills are contrasted with difficulties with coordination and understanding facial expressions and other nonverbal cues.

- Visual perceptual/visual motor deficit: Difficulty interpreting what a person sees, making it hard for a student to copy a picture or words on a page or screen. It can also make it easy for a student to lose his or her place when reading.

Most of these and other learning disabilities do not reflect on a student's intelligence. In fact, many students with learning disabilities have a high IQ and are capable of great academic success, provided their instruction and accommodations match their needs.

Problems with Funding and Staffing

Meeting those needs is the crux of the problem. Many school districts do not make funding and staffing a priority for the services and special instruction that disabled students might need. This is true even though more than one in ten public school students have some type of disability.

Per-pupil funding varies widely from state to state and even between nearby communities. Annual costs to educate a non-disabled student range between $4,000 and $10,000, while per-pupil funding for disabled students can climb as high as $20,000 a year. The federal government provides about 10 percent of funds for both types of students, with the rest coming from state and local sources. Each state has its own funding formulas and budget challenges. The same is true with every school board, which is where many parent-school battles are fought.

It is a difficult balancing act: providing a fair and appropriate education for all students, even when the costs for one group of students far surpass those of another. Budget cuts often require sacrifices from all departments. But many school districts have seen cuts in federal dollars that were specifically earmarked for special education. That means the districts must take away from other areas or cut back on services provided to disabled students. And because disabled students represent a costly but smaller percentage of the student body, special education programs are frequent targets of budget-cutting measures.

Experts believe that some special education students require one-on-one teaching and guidance. However, many schools simply do not have the funding to support this.

In Wyandotte County, Kansas, federal and state cuts to special education programs have resulted in fewer materials for disabled students. Those cuts have also reduced the number of paraeducators, specially trained teaching assistants who work with small groups of students needing extra attention. "We used to have money for updated materials and professional development," says longtime special education teacher Vicki Zasadny. "Now we pretty much have money for paper and pencils."[47]

What many schools cannot or do not provide is the additional instruction time students with disabilities need. Schools are often understaffed when it comes to teachers and aides certified to teach disabled students. Zasadny says:

> When we see something like a student unable to make progress in reading, we need to adjust something to help them.
>
> But we can't increase their time in special education without making the classes larger, and we can't provide more one-on-one attention without more staff. When kids are

struggling to the degree that our special education students are, we really should be working with them in groups of three or less, and some kids really need a group of one. But that just doesn't happen now because we don't have enough staff or enough hours in the day.[48]

Misunderstandings and Bullying

Another common problem facing disabled students and their families is a lack of understanding by educators and students. Because so many learning disabilities are complex and "hidden," in that they relate to processing challenges in the brain, teachers without special education training may simply lack the awareness to properly serve these students.

Fischer recalls one school in which her son was placed in a class of nondisabled students, which put the teacher in a difficult position. This is a common occurrence and is unfair to the disabled student and the teacher. "I'm thinking, 'How in the world is he going to function, and how is this poor regular-ed teacher going to manage this kid who has very complicated needs?'"

Individual Education Plans

Students with disabilities in kindergarten through twelfth grade are often given an Individualized Education Plan (IEP), which spells out the student's challenges and the means by which the school and teachers will try to accommodate them. A key feature of an IEP is a list of learning goals for the student. IEPs are updated each year, so a typical goal might be to have the student reading on grade level by the end of the school year. To help meet those goals, classroom practices are put in place. A standard IEP requirement might be to have the student's desk near the teacher's desk for easier monitoring of work habits or to see if there are problems that need extra attention. IEPs are usually developed with input from the student, his or her parents, teachers, a school psychologist, guidance counselors, and other concerned parties, such as social workers or school administrators.

Fischer says. "Most regular-ed teachers aren't taught specific information about special education."[49]

Children with certain learning challenges are often labeled as "slow" or "lazy" because they have trouble finishing their work. A teacher who publicly reprimands a student for not doing his or her work opens the door for the student's peers to criticize as well. A study by the National Center for Learning Disabilities reported that 45 percent of parents said their disabled children have been bullied in school because of their disabilities, and 66 percent of those parents believe students with disabilities are bullied more than other kids. Jaylen Arnold, a thirteen-year-old student in Tampa, Florida, struggled with bullying from students due to the uncontrolled sounds and movements he would make because of severe Tourette's syndrome, Asperger's syndrome, and obsessive-compulsive disorder. Despite all that, he has given talks at other schools to help combat bullying. "I was bullied, mocked. They'd call me names. They'd call me a freak, and they'd copy me and laugh and point fingers," he says. "Some people don't realize the effects bullying has on other kids. It can make them do horrible, scary, unthinkable things to themselves. It stunk for me. It was horrible, my worst life period that I went through."[50]

> "Some people don't realize the effects bullying has on other kids. It can make them do horrible, scary, unthinkable things to themselves."[50]
>
> —Jaylen Arnold, a thirteen-year-old student with a disability

Segregating Disabled Students

How a school chooses to provide for disabled students can be seen by some as an example of discrimination and by others as an effort to provide a sound educational environment for all students. Having them in a traditional classroom setting can help teach nondisabled students empathy while providing a positive "normal" experience for disabled students who might otherwise feel like outsiders much of the time. But as Fischer noted, inclusion of disabled students with nondisabled students may not always lead to the best educational outcomes.

Two challenges exist. The first is finding (and training) teachers who want to work with special needs students. Most teachers entering the workforce want to work in a mainstream classroom setting. The additional challenges and requirements of being a special education teacher mean fewer qualified professionals are entering that field. The second challenge is overcoming prejudices from families that have little or no experience with disability. Parents of able-bodied kids sometimes complain that having disabled students in a classroom will somehow hurt the education of their own children who are not disabled.

Too much segregation, however, can also be harmful. In Georgia, for example, parents and the SPLC teamed up to take on the state's practice of placing disabled students in separate wings or buildings within regular schools. Sometimes these areas even have their own entrances, so there is virtually no interaction with the able-bodied student population. One school installed a metal detector for the disabled student entrance but not for the other entrances. Arrangements like this can make kids feel unwelcome at their own school. A disabled student told federal investigators, "School is like a prison where I am in the weird class."[51]

The main issue of the SPLC complaint was that thousands of students could have been integrated with their nondisabled peers without interfering with the educational progress of the traditional students. Federal investigators found that the quality of the education provided to the disabled students was, for the most part, substandard. "We're glad that the Department of Justice has taken action to ensure that these students have equal access to a quality education and hope that the state takes the findings seriously," says Rhonda Brownstein, SPLC legal director. "Too many children are languishing under this discriminatory program."[52]

While most legal challenges have focused on how public schools treat disabled students, there have also been plenty of complaints about private schools discriminating against students with disabilities. Some private schools contend that they are not bound by the same laws that affect public school education. However, the courts have upheld that any school—public or private—that receives federal funds must comply with the ADA and other federal requirements. While many private schools operate exclusively without federal funding, some private institutions do receive federal grants or allow parents to receive certain tax exemptions for sending their children to a private school.

College-Level Challenges

The challenge for students with disabilities is not limited to K–12 schools, however. Getting a college education can, in some cases, prove even more formidable for a person with disabilities. A host of challenges await a disabled student upon arriving on campus. Through secondary school, for example, a student could probably rely on family members, teachers, and other familiar faces to help with schoolwork, intervene if classroom accommodations were not working, or offer moral support. Once they start college, students must learn to become self-advocates—whether or not they have disabilities. But those with disabilities have an added burden: They must be willing to seek out whatever special accommodations they need. And then they have to make sure they receive those services.

A host of challenges awaits disabled students when they arrive at college. They need to be self-advocates and seek out whatever special accommodations they need.

Many institutions are quite progressive in how they accommodate students with disabilities. Student services offices make note takers available or provide students with a professor's lecture notes. Tutors trained in working with certain disabilities are also available, often at no additional cost to the student. But that is not always the case. Many educators simply do not know what services are available for students with disabilities, and the institutions they teach at frequently do not consider the sharing of this information to be a priority. "Learning should be a right, not a luxury," says Jackie Koerner, a Saint Louis University graduate assistant who presented some of her dissertation research on testing options and alternative teaching methods at a conference of college administrators. "Many faculty members say they would love to present these options to students, they just don't know what's appropriate."[53]

Impact of Education Discrimination

Fighting disability discrimination in any educational setting is a worthy battle. A substandard education can make it harder for a person to get a good-paying job that provides a good standard of living. Full-time employment is also needed for many people to receive decent medical insurance that will cover extensive health care costs, wheelchairs, assistive devices, and other needs. One reason why many disabled people are not ready for certain career paths is that they never received the education and training necessary for that line of work. "Despite significant improvements in the access to education, people with disabilities still face barriers to receiving the quality education that they need to succeed in the workforce," says Philip Kahn-Pauli. "Nationally, only 65 percent of students with disabilities graduate high school each year compared to 86 percent of student[s] without disabilities."[54]

> "Despite significant improvements in the access to education, people with disabilities still face barriers to receiving the quality education that they need to succeed in the workforce."[54]
>
> —Philip Kahn-Pauli, policy and practices director of RespectAbility

Identifying Learning Disabilities

A learning disability is a brain-based processing problem that interferes with school performance and sometimes life beyond the classroom. A learning disability can affect how a student learns basic skills, such as reading, writing, or math, as well as higher-level skills, such as organization and abstract reasoning. A learning disability may also affect short-term and long-term memory. Usually, a potential learning disability is first identified by a teacher who sees a student struggling to read, take notes, recall information, pay attention, or follow instructions. A school psychologist may be asked to evaluate the student and diagnose a learning disability if one is present. A student's pediatrician and possibly a neurologist or other specialist may also be consulted, depending on the nature of the suspected disability. Through this process, the student will take a range of tests to help pinpoint the challenge. Tests focus on various aspects of processing, such as measuring how well a student can copy words from the board to a paper or how well a student can verbally express thoughts and ideas. Once a disability is diagnosed, parents and educators must work together on a course of action to help the student learn strategies for success and get treatment if necessary.

The effects of education hurdles can be felt immediately and down the road. Being in a school that does not support students with disabilities can also harm a disabled student's already vulnerable self-esteem. It can lead to behaviors and consequences that may go far beyond the classroom, such as dropping out and engaging in reckless behaviors. And without a thorough education, it can be nearly impossible to have a career that is personally and financially rewarding. This affects society as a whole. Every generation of disabled students that does not receive a quality education is one more generation that struggles for independence. They tend to rely on government assistance and often have poor self-confidence, depression, and other emotional and even physical health problems.

If a society wants all of its citizens to be healthy, educated, and successful, it has to be willing to spend the money and devote resources to help those dealing with disabilities. When given the chance—and that includes the head start of a solid education—individuals with disabilities can become productive citizens, improving society in countless ways.

CHAPTER 5

Reasons for Hope

It can seem hopeless at times to see the slow pace of change in society. But there are positive changes taking place that will improve life for people with disabilities. The adoption of laws that protect people with disabilities from being denied educational opportunities and public access is one example. Meaningful changes have also taken place in the workplace. Employees with disabilities are in higher-profile positions, and employers are reaping the benefits of those hirings. For example, in a study of dozens of companies that hired individuals with intellectual and developmental disabilities (IDDs), 80 percent of them reported a positive experience with their new hires. And about one-third of them said these employees far exceeded their expectations in job performance. "They've hired an effective and enthusiastic employee, and now have lower turnover in those jobs," says Anthony Shriver, founder of Best Buddies International, a nonprofit organization that promotes personal development and employment opportunities for people with disabilities. "The culture of our schools have changed since we began inclusion of people with IDD. Our offices can transform as well."[55]

Technological advances are also bringing significant improvements in daily life. These advances are making it possible for people with disabilities to get around, communicate, and just generally go about daily life in much the same way as do their able-bodied peers. Automakers, for example, are producing cars designed for people with disabilities. Instead of foot pedals, the accelerator and brake are operated with handles. Technology is now allowing people who cannot see or do not have the ability to type the opportunity to use computers through voice-recognition software. Some assistive devices are quite commonplace now. Motorized shopping carts weave through grocery store aisles, and closed captioning is a standard part of most television broadcasts.

Societal attitudes toward people with disabilities are also starting to change. This can be seen in the rising number of people with disabilities on the national stage in politics and business. Texas governor Greg Abbott, for example was paralyzed from the waist down in an accident when he was twenty-six. And corporate chief executive officers, such as David Neeleman of JetBlue and Paul Orfalea of Kinko's, openly share their stories of living with attention-deficit/hyperactivity disorder. Television shows and advertising are also featuring more people with disabilities. For instance, characters with openly acknowledged Asperger's syndrome or the characteristics of the condition have been included

In one study, 80 percent of companies that hired individuals with disabilities reported a positive experience. About one third said they exceeded job performance expectations.

in shows such as *The Bridge*, *The Big Bang Theory*, *Bones*, and *Grey's Anatomy*, among others. In recent years advertisements have included examples such as a little girl in crutches and leg braces dressed as Disney's Princess Elsa in a Target Halloween costume flier. Even Lego finally introduced, in 2016, its first mini figure of a person in a wheelchair. While there is still plenty of work to do and plenty of attitudes to change, there are signs that the fight against disability discrimination is being won.

Opening Doors with Technology

A smartphone puts a world of knowledge and human contact in the palm of a hand, but the device requires some small motor skills that elude many people with disabilities. Text-to-speech features are now standard parts of cell phones and Global Positioning System units. Written words on a screen can be heard with the click of a button or even a verbal command. Modified screens with extra bright backlights or larger characters are available for the visually impaired. Sign language apps can help users communicate with the hearing impaired by quickly showing the signs for thousands of words. And for someone with speech difficulties caused by cerebral palsy or other conditions, there are apps that sort out unintelligible pronunciations to make that person's speech more understandable. The app recognizes the person's individual speech patterns to decode what is said and make it easier for listeners to comprehend.

Technology is also boosting access to education for disabled students everywhere. Gallaudet University used to be the only college for hearing-impaired students in the United States. But Fred Weiner, assistant vice president at Gallaudet, says that services such as computer-aided learning programs for the hearing impaired that were once unique to his school can now be found on campuses around the world. "People who are deaf and hard of hearing have more places to go," Weiner says. "They can select a public college or a private college. They can pick a variety of educational settings. And so it's not just access to the classroom, but it's learning in a broader sense. It's access to cultural institutions like museums, cultural events that's really part of the fabric of learning."[56]

New devices and inventions are also allowing disabled people greater independence than ever before. Someone with Parkinson's disease, for example, may have trouble gripping eating utensils or buttoning shirt buttons because of a hand tremor or muscle weakness. But every year, new products, such as specially weighted utensils or fasteners for buttons, hit the market, turning a disability into a minor nuisance. Engineers are also producing prosthetic arms and legs that improve mobility and independence while also allowing people to enjoy activities that once might have been impossible. Veterans who have lost a limb in combat, for instance, are being fitted with prosthetics that enable them to walk and even run again.

Disabled musicians are also benefiting from technology. Jason Barnes was a drummer in a rock band when he lost an arm after being electrocuted in a workplace accident. After seeing a video of the Musical Cyborgs—robotic musicians who play

Engineers are developing more advanced prosthetic arms and legs that improve mobility, allowing people to enjoy activities that might once have been impossible.

along with human musicians—Barnes contacted Gil Weinberg, the creator of the Musical Cyborgs. Weinberg, who also founded the Center for Music Technology at Georgia Tech, designed a prosthetic arm for Barnes. The arm can pound a snare drum at twenty hits per second—faster than what is possible for human arms. "He's the envy of all kinds of heavy metal drummers that would love to have his speed right now," Weinberg says. "Technology for leg and arm amputees can create all kinds of things, such as running, if you're talking about legs, or drumming, if you're talking about arms."[57]

Role Models

Exceeding expectations in sports is another area where disabled individuals have literally made great strides in recent

Businesses Cater to Customers with Sensory Disabilities

People with autism or other sensory disorders can experience physical pain or heightened anxiety from lights, colors, noise, and other stimuli that might not bother someone without a sensory disorder. This can make going to a store or the movies a challenge. But a growing number of businesses are trying to make their environments more welcoming to people with sensory disorders. Retail stores such as JCPenney and Target have experimented with low-key shopping events in which bright overhead lighting and music are turned down. AMC Theatres has also held sensory-friendly screenings of certain movies, in which the house lights are dimmed, the volume is lower than usual, and patrons are encouraged to walk around if they feel the need. And an NBA Store in New York City opened with a quiet space where people can go for a little peace. Shoppers can also borrow "sensory bags" that include noise-canceling headphones and fidget devices inside. "Our hope is that we will demonstrate how easy it is to make spaces more inclusive, and will inspire other stores to do the same," says Todd Jacobson, the NBA's senior vice president of social responsibility.

Quoted in Raz Robinson, "This NBA Store Is Now More Accessible for People with Sensory Disabilities," Fatherly, April 2, 2018. www.fatherly.com.

years. When the flame is finally extinguished at the end of the Summer Olympics or Winter Olympics and the world watches record-shattering athletes depart from those grand stages, the action does not stop. Shortly after the traditional Olympic Games end, the Paralympic Games begin with a new flame and a new set of sprinters, skiers, and scores of other athletes giving their all at high-level competition. Unlike the Special Olympics, in which participation is the focus, the Paralympics bring out top competitors. That the Paralympics have become such a big deal is but one sign in recent years that the perception of people with disabilities is rapidly changing. "As Paralympians receive more medals, they are viewed by many people, including policy makers, as heroes who have overcome adversity," write occupational therapy professors Marion Gray and Michele Verdonck. "As potential 'heroes,' Paralympic athletes are not only role models for other aspiring athletes, especially for those with a disability, but are also admired by society as a whole for their achievements."[58]

One of those much-admired individuals is Kyle Maynard, a mixed martial arts athlete and entrepreneur who found a legion of fans after climbing Mount Kilimanjaro in Tanzania. The climb was historic because Maynard has had parts of both arms and legs amputated, and he scaled the mountain without prosthetics. "If you have a physical disability, it does not mean that you're weak," he says. "You're not fragile."[59]

Role models for people with disabilities are not limited to athletics and feats of physical strength and endurance. Senator Tammy Duckworth of Illinois became the first disabled woman elected to Congress when the double amputee and army veteran was elected to the House of Representatives in 2013. She was elected to the Senate in 2016, and in 2018 she became the first sitting senator to give birth while in office. On the campaign trail, Duckworth openly talked about her challenges and her desire to raise awareness of disability rights and concerns. "I'm not ashamed I'm in a wheelchair. I earned this wheelchair," she says. "I've always insisted it's not something that we hide."[60]

Other notable role models with disabilities include the late physicist and black hole expert Stephen Hawking, who spent most of his life in a wheelchair due to a rare form of motor neuron disease. His disease made normal speech impossible, so he relied on voice-activated software to communicate. Despite his profound disability, people worldwide viewed Hawking as a brilliant scientist and an inspiring human being.

Overcoming another type of disability was Temple Grandin, whose lifelong struggle with autism led her to become a leading expert on the condition, as well as an author and sought-after speaker. She has been a leading voice in the effort to view challenges such as autism as opportunities to have more viewpoints and abilities shared with society. "The skills that people with autism bring to the table should be nurtured for their benefit and society's," she says, adding that she would decline a cure for autism if one were developed. "I like the really logical way that I think. I'm totally logical. In fact, it kind of blows my mind how irrational human beings are."[61]

Allies of the Disabled

Along with people overcoming their own disability challenges, there is also a long and growing list of allies of the disabled community. Eunice Kennedy Shriver, sister to President John Kennedy, founded the Special Olympics in 1968. Hall of Fame quarterback Dan Marino, who formed a foundation to honor one of his children who has autism, has raised tens of millions of dollars for research. Actor Michael J. Fox, who developed Parkinson's disease at a young age, formed a foundation that is spearheading cutting-edge research into that disease. Other organizations are also having an impact. The Center for Disability Rights, for instance, helps people with disabilities find service organizations in their communities and provides services such as adult day care in several cities. Another organization, the World Institute on Disability, helps people with disabilities achieve employment, greater access to health care, and financial empowerment in a variety of ways.

An increasing number of locally based advocates are also key partners in helping disabled people find jobs and services they need. Communities across the country have agencies specifically created to help employers see past their own preconceived ideas about people with disabilities and hire those people who are eager to work. These agencies help make connections between disabled workers and nonprofits or companies that have jobs that could be filled by people with disabilities. And while the work is important to the hiring organization, it can be a lifesaver to people struggling with a mental, physical, or sensory challenge. "So many of the folks have been told when they were younger, 'Oh, you'll never read. You'll never do this, you'll never do that.' They're reading. They live in the community. They have jobs," says Wendy Keegan. Keegan is director of development at Life Works, a social services organization that helps people with mental and physical challenges in Washington State. "It's that sense of pride that they get with a little bit of support, that they can achieve their goals when they want to achieve their goals."[62]

Depictions in the Media

Fictional characters are also helping by changing perceptions of disabled people. Based on its title alone, a TV show called *Crazy Ex-Girlfriend* would seem to play into the stereotypes that plague people with mental illness. But the series on the CW has actually taken a healthy approach to the subject, featuring a lead character who has been diagnosed with anxiety and depression and is up front in how she deals with her challenges. Other shows are also up front in their depictions of people with disabilities.

The cast of the popular TV series *Speechless* features an actor with cerebral palsy. Not long ago, film and TV gave little attention to disabled characters.

Speechless (on ABC) features an actor with cerebral palsy, and *Switched at Birth* (also on ABC) features deafness as a key part of the story lines.

Not long ago, film and TV gave little attention to disabled characters, let alone addressed the causes of disability in such an up-front manner. In the 2017–2018 television season, 1.8 percent of prime time network show characters had a disability, according to a wide-ranging TV survey by the advocacy group GLAAD. While still not reflective of society at large, the numbers amounted to the highest representation since such research began in 2010.

Varied Job Prospects

Among trends that have the potential to make a real difference in the lives of people with disabilities are efforts to bring these individuals into the workplace. Workplace diversity has become an important goal for many major corporations—and the hiring and promotion of people with disabilities is part of achieving that goal. Starbucks has been a leader in this area. Executive vice president Scott Pitasky says Starbucks tries to look beyond traditional employee profiles to find people who fit Starbucks' philosophy of service and community. "There is no better example than our commitment to hiring people with disabilities," he says. "These talented professionals bring unique experiences that foster innovation and new ideas while contributing to a culture of warmth and true inclusion."[63]

Other companies that have taken an active role in hiring and training disabled workers for a range of career paths include telecommunications giant AT&T, defense contractor Northrop Grumman, and the professional services company Ernst & Young. Employers like these are not doing this as an act of generosity or charity. Their own experiences and years of corporate research suggest that having a diversified workforce—one that includes people with disabilities—leads to profits, innovation, and often greater efficiency in the workplace. Lori B. Golden, abilities strategy leader with Ernst & Young, says:

> We know that diverse teams produce better solutions, so there's a clear performance advantage to bringing together people with all kinds of differences—in gender, ethnicity, orientation, age, background and abilities. Employees with disabilities have higher retention rates, so for many busi-

nesses, there can be a real cost savings through reduced turnover. Studies show that consumers prefer doing business with companies that employ people with disabilities, so there's brand value. Research has also found organizations employing people with disabilities have higher morale and employee engagement, which we know drives profitability. Finally, people with disabilities often have well-honed problem solving skills and a degree of adaptability that are especially valuable in today's fast-changing business environment.[64]

Job Training Opportunities

Universities, community colleges, and vocational training centers are all developing programs specifically targeted at people with disabilities. The goal of such programs is to prepare these people for the workforce by providing training for jobs in the restaurant, janitorial, construction, and other fields.

One of the fastest-growing and most successful such programs is Project SEARCH, which started at Cincinnati Children's Hospital in 1997. The program was designed to meet a growing need for health care workers, especially those in high-turnover jobs such as those that involve sterilizing equipment, cleaning and preparing patient rooms, and transporting or escorting patients within a hospital or rehabilitation center. Within twenty years, Project SEARCH went from one site to almost five hundred programs in forty-eight states and four foreign countries. Participants in the program are usually high school students with disabilities who rotate among various departments at a hospital. They learn specific job skills related to the various departments, but with the help of job coaches, they also learn about résumés,

> "People with disabilities often have well-honed problem solving skills and a degree of adaptability that are especially valuable in today's fast-changing business environment."[64]
>
> —Lori B. Golden, abilities strategy leader with Ernst & Young

The Internet Gives People with Disabilities a Worldwide Platform

Having a disability can be an isolating experience. Mobility can be limited, and it can be difficult to find other people with the same condition and the same challenges. But blogs, podcasts, and online communities are reaching people with just about every type of disability imaginable. Tiffiny Carlson, a prolific blogger about living life to the fullest with a disability, suffered a spinal cord injury as a teenager and has relied on a wheelchair ever since. Connecting online with people who share the challenges of life in a wheelchair can be life changing. "Thanks to smartphones, everyone can blog and share their ideas and tips now," she says. "It's incredible. It makes it easier for everyone to connect and helps many newbies to not feel alone."

Tiffiny Carlson, "Q & A: Behind SCI Life with Tiffiny Carlson," *New Mobility*, December 1, 2017. www.newmobility .com.

job interviews, workplace etiquette, and other work-related and life skill lessons.

Many Project SEARCH graduates go on to work at the hospitals or universities where they trained, while others find work elsewhere in their communities. Many jobs are full time with benefits. "Our goal is 100 percent (job placement)," says Mark Steidl, a project manager with Project SEARCH at UCLA Health. "We place at least 70 percent of the individuals into work after the program."[65]

Staying Optimistic

Though there is still a long road ahead in the fight to end disability discrimination, it helps to look back and see how far things have come. Not that long ago, disabled students were either kept out of public schools or were essentially warehoused in classes that did little to prepare them for life after graduation. Most public buildings had no wheelchair ramps, and only very tall buildings had elevators. Employers would often reject disabled job candidates without even interviewing them. There were few role models of successful people with disabilities in the media, politics, and entertainment.

Having a disability can be challenging enough without the additional burdens placed on individuals by discriminatory practices and a population that still struggles to appreciate a person with a disability as just a person. But awareness is growing, and hope remains strong. "I look forward to a day when we don't have to worry that we might lose our jobs, or be looked down upon as professionals, because we have a different profile of skills, challenges, and abilities than those the world calls 'normal,'" Lynne Soraya says. "That one day, the world will look at us, and see the abilities, rather than the disabilities. Unfortunately, we're not there yet. But I have hope."[66]

SOURCE NOTES

Introduction: The Fight for Disability Rights

1. Quoted in Kendo Rainwater, "Judge: Hamilton County Schools Violated Federal Law in Special Education Case," *Chattanooga (TN) Times Free Press*, July 17, 2017. www.timesfreepress.com.
2. Quoted in Patrick Sisson, "Sen. Duckworth: 'Offensive' Law Would Weaken Landmark ADA," *Curbed*, February 28, 2018. www.curbed.com.
3. Quoted in Susan Brink, "How Is the World Treating People with Disabilities?," NPR, December 18, 2016. www.npr.org.
4. Quoted in Paul Davidson, "Willing and Able: Disabled Workers Prove Their Value in Tight Labor Market," *USA Today*, March 5, 2018. www.usatoday.com.

Chapter 1: Causes and Effects of Disability Discrimination

5. Quoted in Center for an Accessible Society, "The ADA: At a Critical Point," 1999. www.accessiblesociety.org.
6. Danielle S. McLaughlin, "Stop Making Degrading Assumptions About People with Disabilities," *The Blog*, *Huffington Post*, February 22, 2017. www.huffingtonpost.ca.
7. Sarah Blahovec, "Basic Myths About Disability That I Can't Believe We Still Have to Debunk," *The Blog*, *Huffington Post*, April 5, 2016. www.huffingtonpost.com.
8. Laurie Block, "Stereotypes About People with Disabilities," Disability History Museum. 2018. www.disabilitymuseum.org.
9. Marie Harman, "Please Stop Trying to 'Fix' My Disability," *The Mighty* (blog), September 20, 2016. www.themighty.com.
10. Quoted in Valentina Rojas-Posada, "Barnard Students with Disabilities Struggle with Denied Accommodations,

Campus Stigma," *Columbia Spectator*, March 1, 2018. www
.columbiaspectator.com.

11. Lynne Soraya, "Disability, Discrimination, and Disclosure: Being 'Out' in the Workplace," *Psychology Today*, July 21, 2011. www.psychologytoday.com.

12. Frances Ryan, "Two-Thirds of Us Are Uncomfortable Talking to Disabled People: We Need Time, Money and Effort to Get Over the Awkwardness," *New Statesman*, May 8, 2014. www.newstatesman.com.

13. Tiffiny Carlson, "6 Instances of Discrimination People with Disabilities Face Every Day," *The Blog*, *Huffington Post*, December 6, 2017. www.huffingtonpost.com.

14. Quoted in Pam Fessler, "Why Disability and Poverty Still Go Hand in Hand 25 Years After Landmark Law," NPR, July 23, 2015. www.npr.org.

15. Rene Momene, "Negative Stereotypes and Attitudes Linked to Disability," *Atlas Corps Blog*, Atlas Corps, December 18, 2015. www.atlascorps.org.

Chapter 2: Living with a Disability

16. John Morris, "A Solution to Movie Theater Accessibility Problems," Wheelchair Travel, March 29, 2016. www.wheel chairtravel.org.

17. Quoted in *PBS NewsHour*, "25 Years On, Celebrating ADA's Advances While Facing Stubborn Barriers," July 23, 2015. www.pbs.org.

18. Carlson, "6 Instances of Discrimination People with Disabilities Face Every Day."

19. Carlson, "6 Instances of Discrimination People with Disabilities Face Every Day."

20. Quoted in Vantage Mobility, "The Emotional Journey of a Full-Time Wheelchair User," June 3, 2016. www.vantagemobility .com.

21. Quoted in Vantage Mobility, "The Emotional Journey of a Full-Time Wheelchair User."

22. Quoted in Heike Klovert and Maria Feck, "I'm Glad I Don't Need Any Shoes," *Spiegel Online*, November 30, 2016. www .spiegel.de.

23. Jeff Charlebois, "Living with a Disability for Dummies," *Ability Magazine*, June/July 2010. www.abilitymagazine.com.

24. Carlson, "6 Instances of Discrimination People with Disabilities Face Every Day."
25. Carlson, "6 Instances of Discrimination People with Disabilities Face Every Day."
26. Quoted in Matt McKinney, "Woman with Heart Condition Returns to Handicapped Parking Spot to Find Insulting Note on Car," NBC26, April 26, 2017. www.nbc26.com.
27. Valerie Piro, "Applying to College as a Wheelchair User," *Inside Higher Ed*, April 6, 2017. www.insidehighered.com.
28. Quoted in Gwen Smith, "Theater Discrimination Decision Seen as 'Wake-Up Call' on Allergy as Disability," Allergic Living, July 18, 2016. www.allergicliving.com.
29. Charlebois, "Living with a Disability for Dummies."
30. Tom Shakespeare, "A Point of View: Happiness and Disability," BBC, June 1, 2014. www.bbc.com.

Chapter 3: Getting and Keeping a Job

31. Quoted in Ananya Bhattacharya and Heather Long, "America Still Leaves the Disabled Behind," CNNMoney, July 26, 2015. www.money.cnn.com.
32. Quoted in Denver Pratt, "People with Disabilities Can Spend Months, Years Looking for Work in Washington's Smaller Communities," *Seattle Times*, December 31, 2016. www.seattletimes.com.
33. Quoted in David Crary, "25 Years On, Act Has Changed Millions of Lives," *San Diego Union-Tribune*, July 15, 2015. www.sandiegouniontribune.com.
34. Quoted in Katie Sola, "Discrimination Against Disabled Applicants Sadly 'Not Surprising': NDRN Director," *Forbes*, November 3, 2015. www.forbes.com.
35. Rebecca Ratcliffe, "I Don't Think Employers See What Disabled People Can Do," *Guardian* (Manchester), October 3, 2017. www.theguardian.com.
36. Quoted in Sola, "Discrimination Against Disabled Applicants Sadly 'Not Surprising.'"
37. Peggy Klaus, "A Chance to See Disabilities as Assets," *New York Times*, February 4, 2012. www.nytimes.com.
38. Quoted in Fessler, "Why Disability and Poverty Still Go Hand in Hand 25 Years After Landmark Law."

39. Quoted in Fessler, "Why Disability and Poverty Still Go Hand in Hand 25 Years After Landmark Law."
40. Soraya, "Disability, Discrimination, and Disclosure."
41. Quoted in Kim Isaacs, "Should You Disclose a Disability on Your Resume?," Monster.com, 2018. www.monster.com.
42. Quoted in Isaacs, "Should You Disclose a Disability on Your Resume?"
43. Quoted in Aimee Picchi, "Americans with Disabilities Still Can't Land Jobs," CBS News, July 26, 2017. www.cbsnews.com.
44. Quoted in Picchi, "Americans with Disabilities Still Can't Land Jobs."

Chapter 4: Challenges in Education

45. Quoted in Southern Poverty Law Center, "Students with Disabilities Encounter Discrimination in New Orleans Schools," March 11, 2014. www.splcenter.org.
46. Quoted in Southern Poverty Law Center, "Students with Disabilities Encounter Discrimination in New Orleans Schools."
47. Quoted in Amanda Litvinov, "How Congress' Underfunding of Special Education Shortchanges Us All," National Education Association, May 19, 2015. www.educationvotes.nea.org.
48. Quoted in Litvinov, "How Congress' Underfunding of Special Education Shortchanges Us All."
49. Quoted in Southern Poverty Law Center, "Students with Disabilities Encounter Discrimination in New Orleans Schools."
50. Quoted in WLOX, "Teen with Disabilities Shares Pain of Being Bullied," 2014. www.wlox.com.
51. Quoted in Southern Poverty Law Center, "After SPLC Complaint, DOJ Finds Georgia Program Violates Disabilities Act," July 23, 2015. www.splcenter.org.
52. Quoted in Southern Poverty Law Center, "After SPLC Complaint, DOJ Finds Georgia Program Violates Disabilities Act."
53. Quoted in Allie Grasgreen, "Dropping the Ball on Disabilities," *Inside Higher Ed*, April 2, 2014. www.insidehighered.com.
54. Quoted in Picchi, "Americans with Disabilities Still Can't Land Jobs."

Chapter 5: Reasons for Hope

55. Quoted in Elizabeth Picciuto, "Hiring People with Disabilities Isn't Just the Right Thing to Do—It's Good for Business," *Daily Beast*, October 27, 2014. www.dailybeast.com.
56. Quoted in *PBS NewsHour*, "25 Years On, Celebrating ADA's Advances While Facing Stubborn Barriers."
57. Quoted in *PBS NewsHour*, "25 Years On, Celebrating ADA's Advances While Facing Stubborn Barriers."
58. Marion Gray and Michele Verdonck, "The Paralympics Is Changing the Way People Perceive Disabilities," Conversation, September 18, 2016. www.theconversation.com.
59. Quoted in Wyatt Massey, "The ADA at 25: What's Next for Disability Rights?," CNN, January 24, 2015. www.cnn.com.
60. Quoted in Beth Winkle, "Our New Illinois Senator Uses a Wheelchair," *Easterseals Blog*, Easterseals, 2018. www.easterseals.com.
61. Temple Grandin, "About Temple Grandin," Temple Grandin, Ph.D., 2012. www.templegrandin.com.
62. Quoted in Pratt, "People with Disabilities Can Spend Months, Years Looking for Work in Washington's Smaller Communities."
63. Quoted in Sarah Blahovec, "Why Hire Disabled Workers? 4 Powerful (and Inclusive) Companies Answer," *Huffington Post*, February 24, 2016. www.huffingtonpost.com.
64. Quoted in Blahovec, "Why Hire Disabled Workers? 4 Powerful (and Inclusive) Companies Answer."
65. Quoted in Lauren Appelbaum, "#RespectTheAbility Campaign: Spotlight on UCLA Medical Center," RespectAbility, February 17, 2017. www.respectability.org.
66. Soraya, "Disability, Discrimination, and Disclosure."

ORGANIZATIONS AND WEBSITES

ACLU Disability Rights

125 Broad St., 18th Floor

New York, NY 10004

website: www.aclu.org/issues/disability-rights

The site highlights key issues in disability rights and provides update information on current and past court cases, as well as changes in legislation or policies that may become the subject of a lawsuit down the road. The site also includes samples of letters constituents can use to write their elected leaders and other decision makers.

Americans with Disabilities Act

US Department of Justice

950 Pennsylvania Ave. NW

Civil Rights Division

Disability Rights Section

Washington, DC 20530

website: www.ada.gov

Learn more about the history of this landmark legislation and what issues it covers. The site includes regulations, building design standards, updates on ADA cases, and information about how to file an ADA complaint or how to comply with ADA requirements.

Disability Rights Education and Defense Fund (DREDF)

3075 Adeline St., Suite 210

Berkeley, CA 94703

website: https://dredf.org

Get the latest information on legislative and courtroom battles for greater disability rights and how changes in the law and court rulings affect individuals with disabilities and their caregivers. The DREDF is a leading voice for disability rights and a longtime resource for people seeking answers or guidance on a wide range of disability issues.

Disability Rights International (DRI)

1666 Connecticut Ave. NW, Suite 325
Washington, DC 20009
website: www.driadvocacy.org

The DRI promotes human rights and the full participation in society of disabled people around the world. Learn about disability discrimination, human rights abuse cases, and how laws to protect disabled people are (or are not) being enforced. There are also opportunities to help support the work of the DRI.

Individuals with Disabilities Education Act (IDEA)

Office of Special Education Programs
US Department of Education
400 Maryland Ave. SW
Washington, DC 20202
website: https://sites.ed.gov/idea

The IDEA site is for students, parents, teachers, and others interested in learning more about the federal government's programs for special education students. The site also has resources and ideas for teachers and parents to help students learn more and develop a positive attitude toward school.

Institute for Community Inclusion

website: www.communityinclusion.org

This comprehensive site includes definitions and characteristics of many disabilities, how to screen for them, how they affect education and work performance, and where people can go to learn even more about each disability.

Learning Disabilities Association of America

4156 Library Rd.
Pittsburgh, PA 15234
website: https://ldaamerica.org

Find strategies and solutions to learning disability challenges, as well as other resources for people with learning disabilities, their teachers, and their families. The site includes information about learning disability assessments for children and adults, contacts in each state, and updates on legislation affecting learning disability education.

US Equal Employment Opportunity Commission (EEOC)

131 M St. NE
Washington, DC 20507
website: www.eeoc.gov

Discover the guidelines the EEOC uses to determine if a disabled worker or job candidate has been treated unfairly. Learn what accommodations employers should provide and how to file a complaint if the accommodations are not made. The site also includes statistics about the EEOC and other information that is useful for employees and employers alike.

Books

Ian Brittain, *The Paralympic Games Explained*. London: Routledge, 2016.

Gail Saitz, *The Power of Different: The Link Between Disorder and Genius*. New York: Flatiron, 2018.

Karen L. Simons, *The Official Autism 101 Manual*. New York: Skyhorse, 2018.

Julie Smart, *Disability, Society, and the Individual*. Austin, TX: Pro Ed, 2015.

Internet Resources

ADA National Network, "An Overview of the Americans with Disabilities Act," 2017. www.adata.org/factsheet/ADA-overview.

Tiffiny Carlson, "6 Instances of Discrimination People with Disabilities Face Every Day," *The Blog*, *Huffington Post*, December 6, 2017. www.huffingtonpost.com/tiffiny-carlson/discrimination-people-disabilities-_b_4509393.html.

Luticha Doucette, "If You're in a Wheelchair, Segregation Lives," *New York Times*, May 17, 2017. www.nytimes.com/2017/05/17/opinion/if-youre-in-a-wheelchair-segregation-lives.html.

Naomi Gingold, "People with 'Invisible Disabilities' Fight for Understanding," NPR, March 8, 2015. www.npr.org/2015/03/08/391517412/people-with-invisible-disabilities-fight-for-understanding.

INDEX